THE CHILDREN'S
Book of Heroes

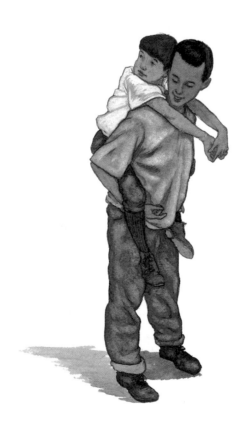

EDITED BY
William J. Bennett

ILLUSTRATED BY
Michael Hague

SIMON & SCHUSTER

THE CHILDREN'S
Book of Heroes

SIMON & SCHUSTER
Rockefeller Center
1230 Avenue of the Americas
New York, NY 10020

SIMON & SCHUSTER and colophon are registered
trademarks of Simon & Schuster Inc.

Designed by Amy Hill

Manufactured in the United States of America

1   3   5   7   9   10   8   6   4   2

Library of Congress Cataloging-in-Publication Data
The children's book of heroes / edited by William J. Bennett ;
illustrated by Michael Hague.
p.   cm.
Summary: Presents a collection of poems, traditional tales, and
both fictional and true stories about all kinds of heroes.
1. Heroes—Literary collections.   [1. Heroes—Literary
collections.]   I. Bennett, William J.   II. Hague, Michael, ill.
PZ5.C43553   1997
808.8'0352—dc21   96-47191
CIP
AC
ISBN 0-684-83445-6

CONTENTS

My wife, Elayne, helps me with many things, and she helped me with this book. Through her efforts it is a better and more beautiful book—just one of the reasons she is a hero to me, and to John and Joseph.
—W.J.B.

To Minnie Minoso
—M.H.

INTRODUCTION

When I was a boy, adults I knew went to the trouble of helping me find a few heroes. At first, the ones I admired most were not people I knew personally, but figures who nonetheless possessed qualities of human excellence worth striving for: baseball and football players who persevered on and off the field, famous explorers from the pages of history who dared to face the unknown, cowboys from Hollywood Westerns who rode hard and stood up for what deserved to be loved and protected. As I grew older, I learned that heroes could be found closer to home, too—neighbors, friends, and members of my own family. In all of them, there was a certain nobility, a largeness of soul, a hitching up of one's own purposes to higher purposes—to something that demanded endurance or sacrifice or courage or compassion.

Looking back, I see how lucky I was that so many of my teachers thought it was worth their time to help me pick the right kind of heroes. As every parent knows, children imitate what they see and hear. They naturally look for examples to follow. Today's popular culture offers plenty. Countless "stars" and "superstars" are put on pedestals for children to idolize and mimic. The problem is that most are celebrities, not heroes (it has been said that the difference between the two is that while the hero is known for worthy actions, the celebrity is known for being well known). And often, especially in our times, the behaviors for which many celebrities are famous are not worthy of imitation. But little children don't know that. They can't foresee that some pedestals, in time, turn out to be shaky and come crashing down. So it makes a big difference whether or not adults make efforts to point out what actions merit honor and which individuals deserve to be admired.

This book is meant to aid parents in such efforts. Its heroes give young people targets to aim for and examples to follow. Their tales come to life in Michael Hague's charming, magical paintings, which speak to the hearts

and imaginations of children. The combination of a few good stories, Michael's illustrations, and a parent's voice reading aloud is a great way to lift children's thoughts toward what is noble and fine.

Some of these heroes are doers of ancient, famous deeds ("mighty men which were of old, men of renown," as the book of Genesis has it)—shining victors, knights in armor, adventurers on the high seas. Their stories often unfold in far-off places—dusty plains, stormy seas, dungeons dark, castles high. Theirs are tales of epic drama—battles against overwhelming odds, daring rescues, struggles to the death, triumphs of good over evil.

But in truth, most heroes are not men and women of great renown. They live close by and, more often than not, perform deeds noticed by only a few. You'll find those kinds of heroes here, too. They come from every walk of life—boys and girls, mothers and fathers, men and women of God, teachers, a neighbor lending a helping hand, the cop around the corner. They win our admiration by committing the sort of acts every one of us might be called upon to perform—by offering some unseen gesture of compassion, by taking a quiet stand for what is right, by managing to hang on just one minute longer, or perhaps by persevering through a lifetime of struggle and toil.

Some of the heroes in this book are real people. They have lived and breathed, just as you and I. Others tread only the worlds of our imaginations. But factual or fictional, they all put a face on and give a meaning to heroism. They give us a chance to say to children, "Look, there is a person who has done something worth imitating."

It is important to say that to children, because believing in the heroic can help make each and every one of us a little bit better, day in and day out. If our children are to reach for the best, they need to have a picture of the best.

I hope this book helps boys and girls to believe in heroes. I hope it inspires parents and children to look around them and together pick out a few heroes of their own.

Heroes

⁓ WILLIAM CANTON

Our favorite heroes live forever in their stories and in our memories, cheering us forward in our own brave fights.

For you who love heroic things
In summer dream or winter tale,
I tell of warriors, saints, and kings,
In scarlet, sackcloth, glittering mail,
And helmets peaked with iron wings.

They beat down Wrong; they strove for Right.
In ringing fields, on grappled ships,
Singing, they flung into the fight.
They fell with triumph on their lips,
And in their eyes a glorious light.

That light still gleams. From far away
Their brave song greets us like a cheer.
We fight the same great fight as they,
Right against Wrong; we, now and here;
They, in their fashion, yesterday.

9

Opportunity

— EDWARD ROWLAND SILL

It's not the sword you use that makes you a hero. It's how you use the sword.

This I beheld, or dreamed it in a dream:
There spread a cloud of dust along a plain;
And underneath the cloud, or in it, raged
A furious battle, and men yelled, and swords
Shocked upon swords and shields. A prince's banner
Wavered, then staggered backward, hemmed by foes.
A craven hung along the battle's edge,
And thought: "Had I a sword of keener steel—
That blue blade that the king's son bears—but this
Blunt thing—!" he snapt and flung it from his hand,
And lowering crept away and left the field.
Then came the king's son, wounded, sore bestead,
And weaponless, and saw the broken sword,
Hilt buried in the dry and trodden sand,
And ran and snatched it, and with battle shout
Lifted afresh, he hewed his enemy down,
And saved a great cause that heroic day.

About Angels

ADAPTED FROM LAURA E. RICHARDS

Here is a story about a guardian angel who is always close at hand, the kind who watches over you from the moment you come into the world.

"Mother," said the child, "are there really angels?"

"The Bible says so," said the mother.

"Yes," said the child. "I have seen the picture. But did you ever see one, Mother?"

"I think I have," said the mother, "but she was not dressed like the picture."

"I am going to find one!" said the child. "I am going to run along the road, miles and miles and miles, until I find an angel."

"That is a good plan!" said the mother. "And I will go with you, for you are too little to run far alone."

"I am not little anymore!" said the child. "I can tie my own shoes. I am big."

"So you are!" said the mother. "I forgot. But it is a fine day, and I should like the walk."

"But you walk so slowly, with your hurt foot."

"I can walk faster than you think!" said the mother.

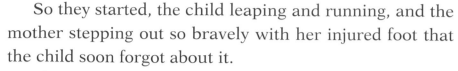

So they started, the child leaping and running, and the mother stepping out so bravely with her injured foot that the child soon forgot about it.

The child danced ahead, and soon he saw a long, silver car coming toward him. In the back sat a splendidly dressed lady. As she moved in her seat, she flashed with jewels and gold, and her eyes were brighter than her diamonds.

The car rolled to a halt at a stop sign.

"Are you an angel?" asked the child, running up beside it.

The lady made no reply, but stared coldly at the child. Then she spoke a word to her driver, and the engine roared. The car sped away in a cloud of dust and fumes, and disappeared.

The dust filled the child's eyes and mouth, and made him choke and sneeze. He gasped for breath and rubbed his eyes, but presently his mother came up and wiped away the dust with the corner of her dress.

"That was not an angel!" said the child.

"No, indeed!" said the mother. "Nothing like one!"

The child danced on again, leaping and running from side to side of the road, and the mother followed as best she could.

By and by the child met a most beautiful young woman, clad in a white dress. Her eyes were like blue stars, and the blushes came and went in her face like roses looking through snow.

"I am sure you must be an angel!" cried the child.

The young woman blushed more sweetly than before. "You dear little child!" she cried. "Someone else said that only last evening. Do I really look like an angel?"

"You *are* an angel!" said the child.

The young woman took him up in her arms, and kissed him, and held him tenderly. "You are the dearest little thing I ever saw!" she said. "Tell me what makes you think so!" But suddenly her face changed.

"Oh!" she cried. "There he is, coming to meet me! And you have soiled my white dress with your dusty shoes, and messed up my beautiful hair. Run away, child, and go home to your mother!"

She set the child down, not unkindly, but so hastily that he stumbled and fell. But she did not see that, for she was hastening to meet her boyfriend, who was coming along the road. (Now if the young woman had only known, he thought her twice as lovely with the child in her arms, but she did not know.)

The child lay in the dusty road and sobbed, till his mother came along, picked him up, and wiped away the tears.

"I don't believe that was an angel, after all," he said.

"No!" said the mother. "But she may be one someday. She is young yet."

"I am tired!" said the child. "Will you carry me home, Mother?"

"Why, yes!" said the mother. "That is what I came for."

The child put his arms around his mother's neck, and she held him tight and trudged along the road, singing the song he liked best. Suddenly he looked up into her face.

"Mother," he said, "I don't suppose *you* could be an angel, could you?"

"Oh, my little one!" said the mother. "I am just your mother who loves you." And she went on singing, and stepped out so happily on her injured foot that she forgot her pain and felt only joy with her young son.

A Prayer at Valley Forge

This story about the Revolutionary War reminds us that in the worst of times, even great men need help. Often, they look to God to find it.

During the Revolutionary War, when Americans were fighting for their freedom, the British army captured Philadelphia. They marched into town with flags flying and bands playing, and made themselves at home for the winter. The fall of Philadelphia was a great blow to the Americans, for in those days it was the capital of the new nation.

But George Washington's army was not strong enough to stop the British forces. Once the king's men were inside the city, the only thing the American general could do was see that they did not get into the countryside to do any mischief. So Washington led his men to Valley Forge, a place just a few miles from Philadelphia. There the American army could spend the winter. It could defend itself if attacked, and it could keep close watch on the British.

It would have been easier to fight many battles than to spend that winter in Valley Forge. It was December, and there was no shelter of any kind. The soldiers bravely set to work building huts for themselves. They made them out of whatever they could find—logs, or fence rails, or just mud and straw. The snow drifted in at the windows, for they had no glass. The cold rain dripped through the roofs. The wind howled through every crack. There were few blankets, and many men slept shivering on the hard ground. Sometimes they sat up all night, crowding around the fires to keep from freezing.

Their clothing was worse than their shelter. The whole army was in rags. Many of the men had no shirts. Even more were without shoes. Wherever they walked, the snow was marked with their blood. Some cut strips from their precious blankets and wound them about their feet to protect them from the freezing ground.

Food was scanty. Sometimes for several days the soldiers went without meat. Sometimes they went even without bread. Around the camp, the groans of men who were sick and starving filled the air. Every evening, when the sun sank, the officers wondered if the army could hold together one more day.

One cold day a Quaker farmer was walking along a creek at Valley Forge when he heard the murmur of a solemn voice. Creeping in its direction, he discovered a horse tied to a tree, but no rider.

The farmer stole nearer, following the sound of the voice. Through a thicket, he saw a lone man, on his knees in the snow.

It was General Washington. His cheeks were wet with tears as he prayed to the Almighty for help and guidance.

The farmer quietly slipped away. When he reached home, he said to his wife, "Hannah, my dear! All is well! The Americans will win their independence! George Washington will succeed!"

"What makes thee think so, Isaac?" she asked.

"I have heard him pray, Hannah, out in the woods today," he said. "If there is anyone on this earth the Lord will listen to, it is this brave man. He will listen, Hannah. Rest assured, He will."

The farmer was right. When at last the harsh winter melted away, and a soft green crept over the hillsides, George Washington's army still lived. Against all odds, it had outlasted the cruel Valley Forge snows. With new hope the patriots marched away behind their brave commander, to fight the British and win their freedom.

Only a Dad

~ EDGAR GUEST

It's not necessarily the big, famous deeds we admire the most. Sometimes, when we pause to appreciate a whole life—all the work, and love, and patient sacrifices for others—we suddenly discover a hero.

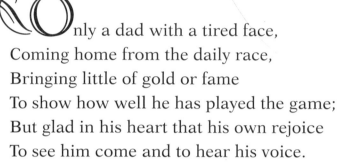

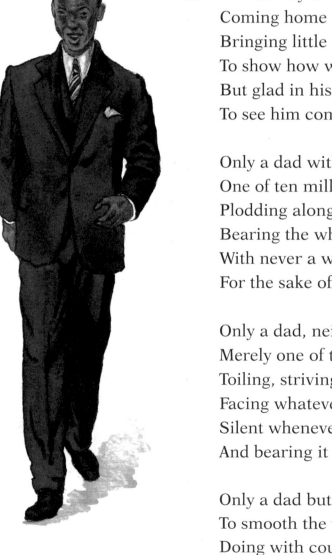

Only a dad with a tired face,
Coming home from the daily race,
Bringing little of gold or fame
To show how well he has played the game;
But glad in his heart that his own rejoice
To see him come and to hear his voice.

Only a dad with a brood of four,
One of ten million men or more
Plodding along in the daily strife,
Bearing the whips and the scorns of life,
With never a whimper of pain or hate,
For the sake of those who at home await.

Only a dad, neither rich nor proud,
Merely one of the surging crowd,
Toiling, striving from day to day,
Facing whatever may come his way,
Silent whenever the harsh condemn,
And bearing it all for the love of them.

Only a dad but he gives his all,
To smooth the way for his children small,
Doing with courage stern and grim
The deeds that his father did for him.
This is the line that for him I pen:
Only a dad, but the best of men.

The Sphinx

ADAPTED FROM A RETELLING BY ELSIE F. BUCKLEY

This famous Greek myth reminds us that heroes use their brains.

It happened in times past that the inhabitants of Thebes were plagued by a very troublesome beast, called the Sphinx. This beast had the face of a woman, but the claws of a lion, and wings of an eagle. It lay crouched on top of a rock, halting all travelers who passed by and posing a riddle. Those who answered it could pass safely, but those who failed were killed. And no one had succeeded in solving the riddle.

One day a traveler named Oedipus came to the seven-gated Thebes, where he found all the people in deep distress and mourning because of the terrible monster. Oedipus stood in the marketplace and talked with the citizens.

"What is this famous riddle that none can solve?" he asked.

"No one can say," they answered. "For he who would solve the riddle must go up alone to the rock where the monster sits. There it chants the riddle, and if he cannot answer, it tears him limb from limb. And if none go up to try the riddle, the monster swoops down on the city and carries off its victims. Our wisest and bravest have gone up, and our eyes have seen them no more. Now there is no one left courageous enough to face the terrible beast."

"I will go up and face this monster," Oedipus said. "It must be a tough riddle indeed if I cannot answer it."

"Oh, overbold and rash," they cried, "why do you think you can succeed, when so many have failed?"

"Better to try and fail than never to try at all."

"Yet, where failure is death, surely a man should think twice?"

"A man can die but once, and how better than in trying to save his fellows?"

They marveled at his answer, and seeing that nothing would turn him from his purpose, they showed him the path to the Sphinx's rock. All the people went with him to the edge of the city with their prayers and blessings. At the gate they left him, for he who goes up to face the Sphinx must go alone, and none can stand by to help him.

He crossed first a river and then a wide plain, where the mountain of the Sphinx stood dark and clear on the other side. Then he prayed to Pallas Athena, the gray-eyed goddess of wisdom, and she took all fear from his heart.

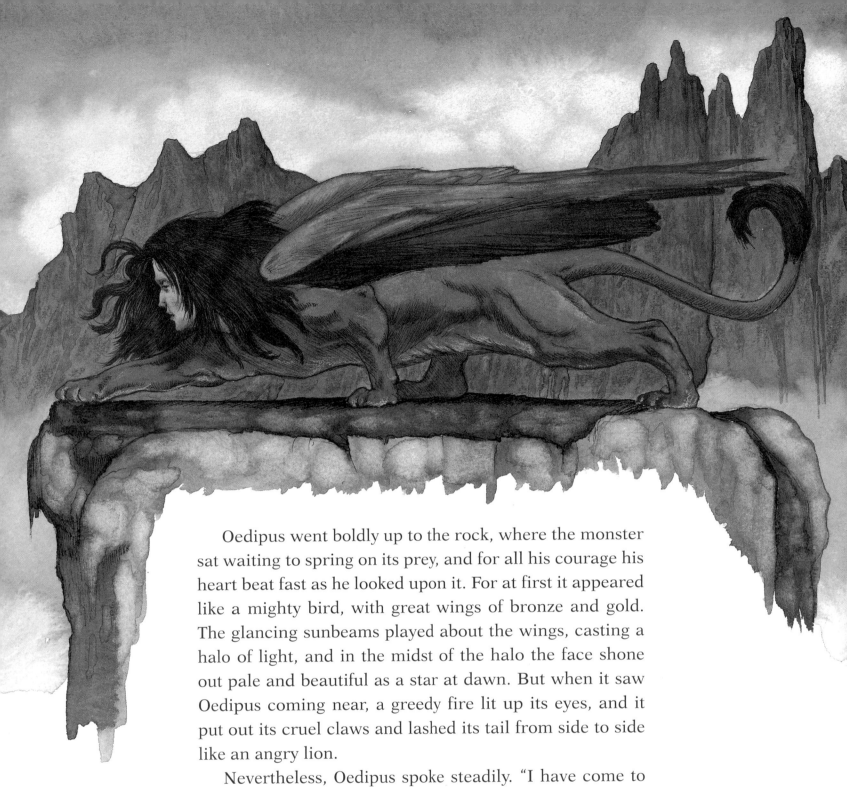

Oedipus went boldly up to the rock, where the monster sat waiting to spring on its prey, and for all his courage his heart beat fast as he looked upon it. For at first it appeared like a mighty bird, with great wings of bronze and gold. The glancing sunbeams played about the wings, casting a halo of light, and in the midst of the halo the face shone out pale and beautiful as a star at dawn. But when it saw Oedipus coming near, a greedy fire lit up its eyes, and it put out its cruel claws and lashed its tail from side to side like an angry lion.

Nevertheless, Oedipus spoke steadily. "I have come to hear your famous riddle and answer it or die."

"Foolhardy manling, a dainty morsel the gods have sent this day, with your fair young face and fresh young limbs."

And it licked its cruel lips.

Then Oedipus felt his blood boil within him, and he wished to slay it then and there.

"Come, tell me your famous riddle, foul Fury that thou art, that I may answer it and rid the land of this curse."

And this is what the monster asked: "At dawn it creeps on four legs. At noon it strides on two. At sunset and evening it totters on three. What is this thing, never the same, yet not many, but one?"

It chanted slowly, its eyes gleaming cruel and cold.

Oedipus thought to himself. "Now or never must my learning and wit stand me in good stead, or in vain have I talked with the wisest men and learned the old secrets of Phoenicia and Greece."

The gods who had given him understanding sent light into his heart, and he boldly answered: "What can this creature be but man, O Sphinx? For, a helpless babe at the dawn of life crawls on his hands and feet. At noontime he walks erect in the strength of his youth. And at evening he supports his tottering limbs with a staff, the prop and stay of old age. Have I not guessed the answer to your famous riddle?"

With a loud cry of despair, and answering him never a word, the great beast sprang up from its seat on the rock and hurled itself over the precipice into the yawning gulf below.

Far away across the plain the people heard its cry, and they saw the flash of the sun on its brazen wings like a gleam of lightning in the summer sky. They sent up a great shout of joy to heaven, and poured out from every gate onto the open plain. Some raised Oedipus on their shoulders and with shouts and songs bore him into the city. Then and there they made him their monarch, for who better to lead them than the slayer of the Sphinx and the savior of the city?

So Oedipus became king of Thebes, and wisely and well did he rule, and for many a long year the land prospered.

Jackie Robinson

Here is the story of an American hero who won his fight using self-control. Often, bravery means keeping your cool and doing the best you can in a bad situation.

More than anything else, Jackie Robinson loved to play baseball. And he was good at it. In fact, he was great. He could run like lightning, and he could hit the ball a mile. And like any other young player, he dreamed of playing baseball in the big leagues, in front of thousands of cheering fans.

But there was one big problem. The year was 1945, and Jackie Robinson was black. It was a time in America when black people were not allowed to do many things that white people could do. That was the rule in baseball too. Black people were not allowed to play on major league teams. They had their own baseball leagues, called the Negro leagues. Jackie played for a Negro league team called the Kansas City Monarchs.

But one day the man who ran a major league team called the Brooklyn Dodgers asked Jackie to come and see him. His name was Branch Rickey.

"I've heard what a good player you are," Mr. Rickey said. "I want you to play for our team."

Jackie could barely believe it. Would he really be the first black baseball player to make it to the big leagues?

"This will not be easy," Mr. Rickey went on. "There will be many, many people who will not want you to play for the Dodgers. Some of the players will call you dirty names. There will be fans in the stands who will yell awful things at you. Even some of the umpires will be against you, and will not give you fair calls."

"I can take it," Jackie said.

"You have to do more than that," Mr. Rickey told him. "You'll have to take it quietly. You cannot shout back. You cannot lose your temper and get into a fight. That's just what they want you to do. It will give them an excuse to throw you out of baseball. No, you must have the guts to fight back another way. The only way you can win this fight is by keeping your temper, and playing the best baseball you can.

You have to show them what a great player you are. That's how you will win this fight."

Jackie thought it over. It would not be an easy thing to do. At last he looked Mr. Rickey straight in the eye.

"I'll do it," he said. "I promise."

Mr. Rickey sent him to practice for a while with a Dodger farm team called the Montreal Royals. Every bad thing that Mr. Rickey had talked about came true—and more. Some of the other players said ugly things to him. Some refused to stand on the same field with him. Newspapers claimed he would not be able to play baseball well enough to stay on a white team. He was locked out of ball-parks. In one town, a policeman even threatened to arrest him if he did not leave the field.

These things hurt Jackie's feelings deeply. Sometimes they made him so angry he wanted to raise his fists and strike back. But he remembered the promise he had made, and he kept his cool.

During Jackie Robinson's first game as a Montreal
Royal, all eyes were on him. He knew how much was riding on that game, and it made him feel weak in the knees.
But when his turn came, he stepped up to the plate and
swung with all his might. The crowd heard the crack of the
bat and watched the ball fly—and fly—and fly—right over
the outfield wall. Jackie rounded the bases, and everyone
knew then that he had come to play great baseball.

The next year, Jackie went to play with the Dodgers. He was in the big leagues at last! But his troubles did not end. In fact, they got only worse. Fans jeered him, and even threatened to harm him. Pitchers threw balls straight at him, trying to hit him. Players shoved him on the field or stepped on his feet at first base, where he played. But through it all, Jackie stayed calm and played great baseball.

One day, one of Jackie's teammates, a shortstop named Pee Wee Reese, trotted across the field to chat with Jackie. He put a friendly hand on Jackie's shoulder while he talked, and a photographer took a picture of the two men together. Newspapers all over the country carried the shot. The message was clear. There were white players who liked Jackie, and knew he was a great player, and were ready to have him on their team. They did not care about the color of his skin.

The more Jackie played, the more respect he won. There were still plenty of people who gave Jackie trouble simply because he was black. But as more and more people watched him play, they saw that he was good enough to be on any team. At the end of his first year with the Dodgers, Jackie was named Rookie of the Year—the best new player in the league.

He had shown the world that the color of his skin did not matter. What mattered was his skill with the bat and the ball, and his courage to lead the way.

Sail On! Sail On!

Sometimes being a hero means having the courage and determination to say,
"Forward!" while the crowd all around you cries, "Turn back!"

Behind him lay the gray Azores,
Behind the gates of Hercules;
Before him not the ghost of shores,
Before him only shoreless seas.
The good mate said: "Now must we pray,
For lo! the very stars are gone;
Speak, Admiral, what shall I say?"
"Why say, sail on! and on!"

"My men grow mut'nous day by day;
My men grow ghastly wan and weak."
The stout mate thought of home; a spray
Of salt wave wash'd his swarthy cheek.
"What shall I say, brave Admiral,
If we sight naught but seas at dawn?"
"Why, you shall say, at break of day:
'Sail on! sail on! and on!'"

They sailed and sailed, as winds might blow,
Until at last the blanch'd mate said:
"Why, now, not even God would know
Should I and all my men fall dead.
These very winds forget their way,
For God from these dread seas is gone.
Now speak, brave Admiral, and say—"
He said: "Sail on! and on!"

36

They sailed, they sailed, then spoke his mate:
"This mad sea shows his teeth tonight,
He curls his lip, he lies in wait,
With lifted teeth as if to bite!
Brave Admiral, say but one word;
What shall we do when hope is gone?"
The words leaped as a leaping sword:
"Sail on! sail on! and on!"

Then, pale and worn, he kept his deck,
And thro' the darkness peered that night.
Ah, darkest night! and then a speck—
A light! a light! a light! a light!
It grew—a star-lit flag unfurled!
It grew to be Time's burst of dawn;
He gained a world! he gave that world
Its watchword: "On! and on!"

David and Goliath

~ ADAPTED FROM A RETELLING BY
J. BERG ESENWEIN AND MARIETTA STOCKARD

Here is one of the world's most beloved heroes, a boy who found his courage in his faith.

Long ago, in the land of Bethlehem, there lived a shepherd boy named David. David was young, but he was also brave. His eye was keen and his hands were strong. Sometimes fierce, wild beasts would creep up the hillside where David watched his sheep, and try to seize a lamb. Then David would rush forward to defend his flock. Sometimes he took his sling and hurled a stone at the beast, and he never missed his mark.

There came a time when the army of the Philistines came marching across the hills to drive the people of Israel away from their homes. King Saul gathered his own army and went out to meet them. David's three oldest brothers went with the king, but David was left at home to tend the sheep. "You are too young," they told him. "Stay in the fields and keep the flocks safe."

Forty days went by, and no news of the battle came. Then David's father called him and said, "Take this food to your brothers in the camp, and see how they are doing."

David set out early in the morning and journeyed up to the hill where King Saul's army was camped. There was a great shouting between the army of the Israelites and army of the Philistines when David arrived. He made his way through the ranks and found his brothers.

As he stood talking with them, silence fell upon King Saul's army. For there on the opposite hillside, where the Philistine army lay, stood a great giant. He strode up and down, his armor glittering in the sun. His shield was as large as a great chariot wheel, and the sight of his mighty sword slashing the air struck terror in the hearts of King Saul's men.

"It is the great giant Goliath," David's brothers told him. "Each day he strides over the hill and calls out his challenge to the men of Israel, but no man among us dares to stand before him."

"What! Are the men of Israel afraid?" asked David. "Will no one go to meet him? Then I will go forth and meet this giant myself. I have no fear of him, for I know God will go with me."

King Saul heard about his words and called David. When he saw that David was only a boy, he tried to talk him out of facing the giant alone. But David had no fear.

"The Lord will keep me safe," he told Saul.

"Very well," said King Saul. "Go, and the Lord be with you!"

Then the king ordered his guards to bring his very own armor and sword for David. But David said, "I cannot fight with these. I am not skilled in their use." He put them down, for he knew that each man must win his battles with his own weapons.

Then he took his staff in his hand. With his shepherd's
bag and sling hanging at his side, he set out from the camp
of Israel. He ran down the hillside and came to a stream.
There he stooped and chose five smooth stones from the
stream, which he dropped into his bag.

The army of King Saul watched in silent wonder from
one hill, while the host of the Philistines watched from the
other. The great giant saw David and strode out to meet
him. When Goliath saw that it was only a boy coming, he
stopped.

"Do the men of Israel mock me by sending a child
against me?" he shouted. "Turn back, or I will give your
flesh to the birds of the air and the beasts of the field!"

But David had no fear in his heart, for he knew that
God was with him. He put his hand into his bag and took
one of the stones from it. He fitted it into his sling, and his
keen eye found the place in the giant's forehead that the
helmet did not cover.

As Goliath rushed forth to meet David, the shepherd drew his sling, and with all the force of his strong right arm, he hurled the stone.

It whizzed through the air and struck Goliath's forehead. His huge body tottered—then fell crashing to the ground. As he lay with his face upon the earth, David ran swiftly to his side, drew forth the giant's own sword, and severed his huge head from his body.

As soon as the army of Israel saw this, they rose with a great shout and rushed down the hillside. When the Philistines saw their greatest warrior slain by this lad, they fled toward their own land, leaving their tents and all their riches behind.

David the shepherd boy became known throughout the land for his bravery and his faith, and years later he became the king of Israel.

Our Heroes

~ PHOEBE CARY

Seeing what is right and doing it, even though the world tempts you to do something else, is the mark of moral courage.

Here's a hand to the boy who has courage
To do what he knows to be right;
When he falls in the way of temptation,
He has a hard battle to fight.
Who strives against self and his comrades
Will find a most powerful foe.
All honor to him if he conquers.
A cheer for the boy who says "NO!"

There's many a battle fought daily
The world knows nothing about;
There's many a brave little soldier
Whose strength puts a legion to rout.
And he who fights sin single-handed
Is more of a hero, I say,
Than he who leads soldiers to battle
And conquers by arms in the fray.

Be steadfast, my boy, when you're tempted,
To do what you know to be right.
Stand firm by the colors of manhood,
And you will o'ercome in the fight.
"The right" be your battle cry ever
In waging the warfare of life,
And God, who knows who are the heroes,
Will give you the strength for the strife.

Honest Abe

Some people grow to be great heroes by doing small, good deeds.

When Abraham Lincoln was a young man in the river town of New Salem, Illinois, he took a job as a clerk in a general store. There he sold the kinds of items frontier settlers needed—everything from buttons and cloth to ax handles and gunpowder.

One day a woman came into the store to buy a few things. Abe bundled her purchases and added up the bill. It came to two dollars and six cents. The woman laid the coins on the counter and, taking her package, wished Abe a good day.

But that evening, when the young clerk closed the store
and sat down to count the day's earnings, he discovered he
had six cents more than he should. He had taken too much
from one of his customers. He realized at once who it was.

"I made a mistake," he said to himself. "I made her pay
six cents too much."

Now even in those days, six cents was not much money.
Many clerks would have shrugged and forgotten it. Abe
was too honest for that.

"The money must be paid back," he decided.

That would have been easy enough if the woman had
lived just around the corner. But as Abe knew, she lived
three miles outside of town. That did not matter. He locked
the store and set out.

It was getting dark outside. The moon climbed the sky and peered down from the clouds at a lone figure trudging through fields and woods.

At last Abe arrived at his customer's house. He knocked on the door, explained what had happened, paid back the six cents, and walked home satisfied.

That was the way the young clerk treated people—he always dealt fair and square with friends and strangers. Stories about his character spread among the folk of New Salem. They spoke of Abe Lincoln with warm, admiring smiles.

And years later, after he became President of the whole United States, they liked to remember him by the nickname he had earned in their town—"Honest Abe."

How the Animals
Got Sunlight

This Native American tale is about trying against the odds, even when others have already tried and failed. Such perseverance sometimes makes heroes.

Once this part of the world was continually dark, and all the animals kept fumbling around and knocking into one another, and they never knew where they were in such blackness. Finally they called a great council to decide how to solve the problem.

"What we need is light," the Owl said. The Owl presided over the meeting because he could see better in the dark than the other animals.

"That's right! We need light," everyone cried. "But where do we get it?"

"It's not an easy thing," the Owl warned. "They say there is light on the other side of the world. But that's a long way away. The journey will be dangerous. Whoever goes may well never come back."

"Then who should go?" everyone cried at once. "Who will risk the journey?"

There was a long silence. All the birds and beasts shuddered in the blackness.

At last they heard a lowly voice.

"I'll try," the Possum offered. "I have a long, bushy tail. I can wrap some light inside its fur and carry it home behind me."

So the Possum set out alone, traveling to the east. He walked for days and days across the black earth, never knowing where he really was, until finally he began to see a little glow in the sky.

He hurried toward it, and it grew lighter and lighter. Soon it was so bright it hurt his eyes, and he had to squint to keep it from blinding him. And even today, possums often close their eyes in narrow slits, so that they look as though they are sleeping.

Finally, when he'd gone all the way to the other side of the world, the Possum found the sun. He grabbed a piece as fast as he could and wrapped it up in his long, bushy tail, and turned for home.

But the journey home was just as long, of course, and the piece of sun was too hot and bright for poor Possum. It burned all the fur off his tail, and fell onto the ground. That's why, today, Possum's tail is long and bare.

"Possum tried and failed," all the animals cried when he came home in darkness. "Now we'll never have any light."

"I'll try now," offered the Vulture. "Maybe this journey calls for someone with wings."

So the Vulture flew east, and finally he came to the sun. He dived and snatched a piece of it in his claws.

"Possum tried to carry the sun with his tail and dropped it," he told himself. "I'll try carrying it on my head."

Vulture set the piece of sun on his head and turned for home, but the sun was so hot that before long it had burned away all the feathers on his crown. He grew dizzy and lost his way, and began wandering around and around until the piece of sun tumbled to the ground. That is why today a vulture's head is bald, and you'll still see him drifting in circles high overhead.

"Now we're truly finished," the animals cried when Vulture returned in darkness. "Possum and Vulture tried as best they could, but it wasn't enough."

"Maybe we need to try one more time," a tiny voice rose from the weeds. "I'll go this time."

"Who is that?" the animals asked. "Who said that?"

"It's me, Old Lady Spider. I know I'm small and slow, but perhaps I'm the one who can make it."

Before she started, she gathered a bit of wet clay, and with her eight tiny hands she made a little pot.

"Possum and Vulture had nothing to carry the sun in," she said. "I'll put it in this pot."

Then she spun a thread and fastened the end to a rock.

"The sun's bright light hurt Possum's eyes, and its heat made Vulture so dizzy he lost his way," she said. "But I'll follow this thread home."

So she set out, traveling east, spinning her thread behind her as she walked. When she reached the sun, she pinched off a small piece and put it in her clay pot. It was still so bright she could hardly see, but she turned and followed her thread home.

She came walking out of the east all aglow, looking like the sun itself. And even today, when Old Lady Spider spins her web, it looks like the rays of the rising sun.

She reached home at last. All the animals could see for the first time. They saw how tiny and old Spider was, and they wondered that she could make the journey alone. Then they saw how she had carried the sun in the little pot, and that was when the world learned to make pots out of clay and set them in the sun to dry.

But Old Lady Spider had had enough of being so close to the sun. That is why, today, she spins her web in the early morning hours, before the sun is too high and hot.

The Star Jewels

— ADAPTED FROM THE BROTHERS GRIMM

This beautiful little story echoes the words we find in the Gospel of Matthew: "I was hungry and you gave me food. . . . I was naked and you clothed me."

A little girl once lived all alone with her old grandmother on the borders of a forest. They were so poor that they were scarcely able to buy food to eat or clothes to cover them.

"Never mind, Granny," the little girl would say. "Someday I will be big enough to work, and then I will earn so much that I will be able to buy everything that we need, and to give something to other poor folk as well."

One day the child went off into the forest to gather sticks. These she hoped to sell for a few pennies in the town over beyond the hill. She was to be gone all day, so she took with her into the forest a bit of bread, which was all they had left to eat.

It was winter, and the air was bitterly cold. The child wrapped her little shawl about her and ran on as fast as she could. She was hungry, but she intended to save her crust until after the sticks were gathered.

Just as she reached the edge of the forest she met a boy
even smaller than herself, and he was crying bitterly.

The little girl had a tender heart. She stopped and
asked the child why he was weeping.

"I am weeping," he answered, "because I am hungry."

"Have you had nothing to eat today?" she asked.

"I have had nothing, and I am starving, for I do not
know where to go for food."

The little girl sighed. "You are probably hungrier than I
am," she said, and she took the crust from her pocket and
gave it to the boy. Then she again hurried on.

A little farther on, she met another child, who was even more miserable looking than the first, for this child seemed almost frozen with cold. Her clothing hung about her in rags, and her skin looked blue through the holes.

"Ah," cried she, "if I had but a warm little dress like yours! Help me, I pray you, or I will certainly die of cold."

The good little girl was filled with pity. "I have both a dress and a shawl," she thought. "I will give one of them to this poor child."

She took off her dress and gave it to the child, and then wrapped the shawl closely about her shoulders. In spite of the shawl she felt very cold. Still, she was near the place where the sticks were to be found, and as soon as she had gathered them, she would run home again.

She hastened on, but when she reached the place where the sticks were, she saw an old woman already there, gathering up the fallen wood. The old woman was so bent and poor and miserable looking that the little girl's heart ached for her.

"Oh, oh!" groaned the old woman. "How my poor bones do ache. If I had but a shawl to wrap about my shoulders I would not suffer so."

The child thought of her own grandmother and of how she sometimes suffered, and she took pity on the old woman.

"Here," said she. "Take my shawl," and slipping it from her shoulders, she gave it to the old woman.

And now she stood there in the forest with her arms and shoulders bare, and with nothing on her but her little shift. The sharp wind blew about her, but she was not cold. She had eaten nothing, but she was not hungry. She was fed and warmed by her own kindness.

She gathered her sticks and started home again. It was growing dark and the stars shone through the bare branches of the trees. Suddenly an old man stood beside her. "Give me your sticks," said he, "for my hearth is cold, and I am too old to gather wood for myself."

The little girl sighed. If she gave him the sticks she would have to stop to gather more. Still, she would not refuse him. "Take them," she said, "in heaven's name."

No sooner had she said this than she saw it was not an old man who stood before her, but a shining angel.

"You have fed the hungry," said the angel. "You have clothed the naked, and you have given help to those who asked it. You shall not go unrewarded. See!"

At once a light shone around the child, and it seemed to her that all the stars of heaven were falling through the bare branches of the trees. But these stars were diamonds and rubies and other precious stones. They lay thick upon the ground. "Gather them together," said the angel, "for they are yours."

Wondering, the child gathered them together—all that she could carry in the skirt of her little shift.

When she looked about her again, the angel was gone, and the child hastened home with her treasure. It was enough to make her and her old grandmother rich. From then on they lacked for nothing. They were able not only to have all they wished for, but to give to many who were poor. So they were not only rich, but beloved by all who knew them.

Mother Teresa

Great heroes aren't only in stories of old and history books. They live and breathe and walk among us. Here is a modern-day heroine who has devoted her life to helping the needy all over the world.

In faraway India, in a city called Calcutta, there lives a woman named Mother Teresa. She is a small woman. Her back is bent with age. Her hands are rough from a lifetime of toil. Her face is wrinkled, but her eyes are steady and bright.

Mother Teresa is a nun, a woman of God. She lives in a large house with other women, who call one another "Sister," for they are like a family. They all have given their lives to God and try to do His work.

If you could go visit Mother Teresa and spend a day with her, what would you see?

She rises from bed very early in the morning, long before the sun rises. She says her prayers, eats her breakfast, and does her chores with the sisters. Then she leaves her house and goes into the streets.

Follow her, and you will see her walk into parts of the city where the buildings are dirty, the streets are full of trash, and the people wear sad, tired looks on their faces. She sees a child, perhaps no older than you, sitting against the wall. His clothes are ragged and his face is covered with dirt. He does not have a home. He does not know where his parents are.

Mother Teresa stops. She takes him by the hand. She wipes the dirt off his face and the tears from his eyes. She leads him to a place where the sisters will give him a bath and new clothes. Then they will try to find a family who will love him and take him into their home.

"A child is a gift of God," Mother Teresa says.
"Every child is here to love and be loved."

Follow Mother Teresa now as she walks more streets. She goes to the house of a woman who is sick. This woman has nobody to care for her. No one wants to come near her, for fear of catching her sickness. Mother Teresa bends over her bed. She gives her some medicine. She washes the places where her skin shows signs of disease. Then she cleans the poor woman's room and opens the windows to let in the fresh air.

"God has given us each a lighted lamp," Mother Teresa says. "It is our job to keep it burning. We can keep it burning only by pouring oil inside. That oil comes from our own acts of love."

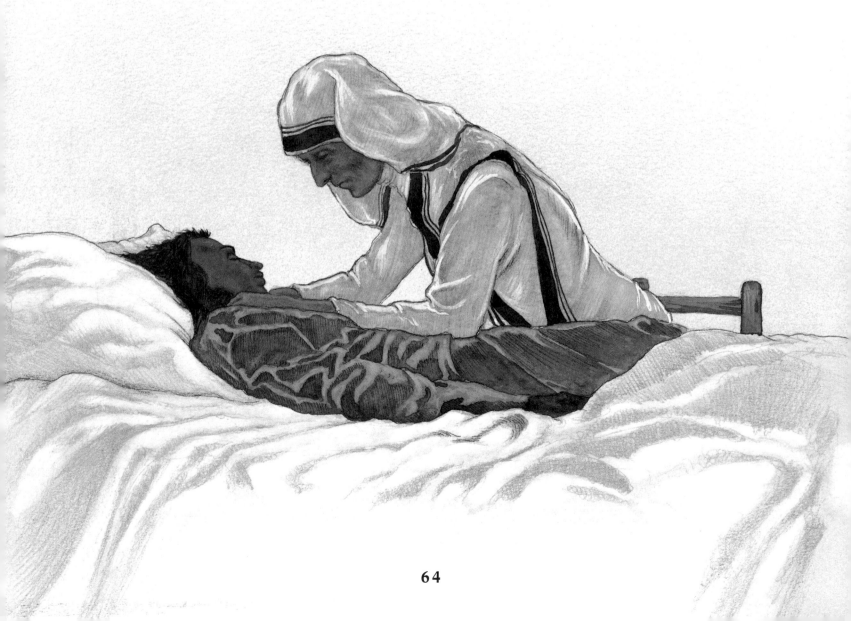

Follow Mother Teresa farther, and watch her go to the house of a family that has not eaten all day. The children's faces are thin from hunger. Mother Teresa gives this family some rice, and their eyes light up. Then the mother of the family does something wonderful. She takes the rice and divides it into two parts. She takes one half and carries it to the family next door.

"They are hungry, too," she tells Mother Teresa.

Mother Teresa smiles. "We call these people poor," she says, "but they are rich in love!"

Follow Mother Teresa just a little while longer, and you see her walk up to an old, old man in the street. He too looks sad and tired.

Mother Teresa lays a hand on his shoulder. "How are you doing?" she asks kindly.

The stranger is surprised, but his face lights up in a smile.

"It has been so long since I felt the warmth of another's hand!" he cries. "It has been so long since anyone cared to speak to me!"

Mother Teresa talks to him for a while, giving him comfort.

"The worst hunger of all is the hunger for love," she tells you as she walks on her way. "The worst sickness is the feeling that no one wants you."

If you came back another day and followed Mother Teresa again, you might see her get on a plane and fly far away, to other lands. You might see her visit the people of a country where there has been a terrible earthquake. You might see her travel to a place torn by war. Or you might find her visiting some of the sisters who do the same kind of work in their own countries as Mother Teresa does in India.

If you could travel with Mother Teresa, you would see that a wonderful thing has happened. You would meet many people who have seen what Mother Teresa is doing. They have seen her helping the poor and the sick, one person at a time. And they have decided to act like Mother Teresa. In their own countries, in their own cities, they take care of people who have no one else to help them. These are the Missionaries of Charity. You can find them all over the world.

And so this one little woman who walks the streets in India, trying to help one person at a time, has really helped thousands and thousands of people all over the world. It is a kind of miracle.

If you ask Mother Teresa, she will tell you that it is not her doing. "It is God's work that has been done, not my work," she says. "I am just God's pencil. That is all I am. I am His tiny pencil, and He writes through me. He uses me to write what He likes."

She smiles as she tells you good-bye. But she stops to say one more thing. What is it she wants to tell you? It is this.

"Let everything you do be something beautiful for God," she says.

The Knights of the Silver Shield

~ RAYMOND M. ALDEN

Sometimes being a hero means resisting the call to glory elsewhere and standing fast at your post.

Once in a land far away there was a dark and dangerous forest, where many cruel giants lived. But in the middle of this forest stood a splendid castle. And inside the castle lived a company of knights, who fought the cruel giants whenever they could.

Each of these knights had a silver shield that did something quite wonderful. When a new knight first received his shield, its surface looked cloudy and dull. As the knight began to do service against the giants, his shield grew brighter and brighter, until he could see his face reflected on its surface. But if the knight proved to be lazy or cowardly, his shield grew more and more cloudy, until he became ashamed to carry it.

But this was not all. When any one of the knights won a very great victory, not only did his silver shield grow brighter, but anyone looking into its center could see something like a golden star shining in its very heart. Winning his star was the greatest honor a knight could achieve.

There came a time when the giants in the forest gathered themselves together to battle the knights. All the knights in the castle made ready to go out and fight them.

Now, there was one young knight named Sir Roland. Though he was still quite young, his shield had already begun to shine enough to show that he was brave. He could not wait to ride forth and battle the giants, to prove what knightly stuff he was made of.

But the lord of the castle came to him and said: "One brave knight must stay behind and guard the castle gate. Since you are the youngest, I have chosen you, Sir Roland."

Sir Roland was so disappointed that he bit his lip and closed his helmet over his face so the other knights would not see it. For a moment he felt as if he must reply angrily to the commander and tell him it was not right to leave so sturdy a knight behind. But he struggled against this feeling and went quietly to look after his duties at the gate.

Soon all the other knights marched out in their flashing armor. The lord of the castle stopped only to give Sir Roland the key to the gate. He told him to keep guard until they all returned, and to let no one enter. Then the knights rode into the shadows of the forest and were lost to sight. Sir Roland stood looking after them unhappily.

A long time passed. At last Sir Roland saw one of the knights come riding along the path to the castle, and he walked out on the drawbridge to meet him.

"I have been hurt and cannot fight anymore," said the knight. "I can watch the gate for you, if you would like to go back in my place."

At first Sir Roland's heart leaped with joy. But then he thought better, and he said:

"I would like to go, but a knight belongs where his commander has put him."

The knight was ashamed when he heard this, and he turned around and went back into the forest.

Sir Roland kept guard silently for another hour, worrying about his friends. Then an old woman came down the path to the castle, and stopped to rest on the other side of the moat.

"I have been past the hollow in the forest where the battle is going on," she called. "The knights are faring badly. I think you had better go help your friends."

"I would like to go," Sir Roland answered, "but I am set to guard the castle gate, and I cannot leave."

"Oh, I see." The old woman laughed. "You are one of the kind of knights who like to keep out of the fighting. You are lucky to have so good an excuse for staying home."

Sir Roland was angry then and wanted to go help his friends more than ever. But instead he shut the gate so he would not have to hear the old woman's laughs.

It was not long before he heard someone else calling outside. He opened the gate and saw standing at the other end of the drawbridge a little old man in a long black cloak.

"Sir Roland!" he called. "You should not be wasting time here when the knights are having such a hard struggle against the giants. Listen to me! I have brought you a magic sword."

And he drew from under his cloak a wonderful sword that flashed as if it were covered with diamonds. "Nothing can stand before this sword!" he called. "Take it into battle, and when you lift it the giants will fall back, and your friends will be saved!"

Sir Roland believed this man must be a friendly magician. He reached out his hand toward the sword, and the little old man started onto the drawbridge. But just then Sir Roland remembered his orders and cried out, "No!"

The little old man waved the sword in the air and cried, "But it is for you! Take it, and win the victory!"

Sir Roland was afraid that if he looked any longer, he would not be able to stay inside the castle. So at once he drew up the drawbridge.

Then, as he looked across the moat, he saw a wonderful thing. The little old man threw off his black cloak, and suddenly he began to grow bigger and bigger, until he was a giant as tall as any tree in the forest!

Sir Roland knew at once that this must be one of their giant enemies, who had changed himself into a little old man through some magic power, so that he might trick his way into the castle while the other knights were away. The giant shook his fist across the moat and went angrily back into the forest.

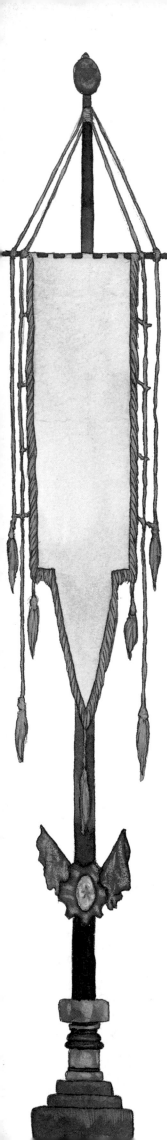
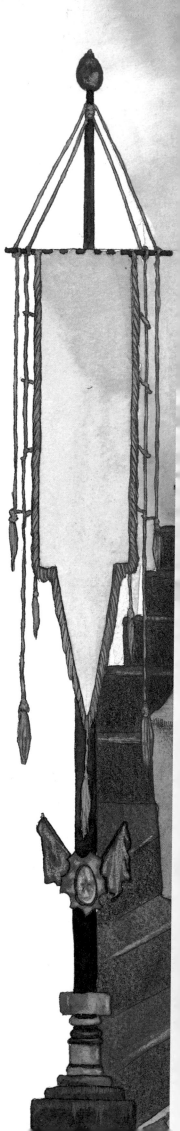

A moment later, Sir Roland heard his master's bugle and shouts of victory. The knights came riding back. They were dusty and bloodstained and weary, but they had won the battle.

Sir Roland greeted them all as they passed over the drawbridge, and then followed them into the great hall of the castle. The lord of the castle took his place on the highest seat, and Sir Roland came forward to return the key to the gate. As he approached, one of the knights cried out:

"The shield! Sir Roland's shield!"

For there, in the very center of Sir Roland's shield, shined the golden star!

"Speak, Sir Knight," said the commander, "and tell us all that has happened today at the castle. Have you been attacked? Did you fight the giants alone?"

"No, my lord," said Sir Roland. "Only one giant has been here, and he went away silently when he found he could not enter." Then he told them everything that had happened that day.

When he had finished, the knights all looked at one another, but no one spoke a word. At last the lord of the castle spoke.

"Men make mistakes," he said, "but our silver shields are never mistaken. Sir Roland has fought and won the hardest battle of all today."

The others rose and gladly saluted Sir Roland, who was the youngest knight who ever carried the golden star.

The Minotaur

These two brave heroes were afraid of the danger they faced—one can almost hear their hearts beating. They chose to do the right thing anyway.

Long ago, in ancient Greece, the city of Athens lived under a sad, cruel curse. Once every seven years, a ship with black sails entered its port. The ship came from the island of Crete, which was ruled by the great King Minos, the Athenians' dreaded enemy. Each time it came, the vessel took seven young men and seven young women from Athens, and then sailed away again.

A terrible fate awaited these poor captives when the black-sailed ship reached Crete. There King Minos kept a strange prison, a kind of maze, called the Labyrinth. It was full of dark winding ways, cut in the solid rock, and inside lived a horrible monster called the Minotaur. This monster had the body of a man, but his head was the head of a bull, his teeth the teeth of a lion, and he devoured everyone he met. It was the fate of the Athenian youth to be thrown into the Labyrinth, to meet the awful Minotaur.

Every seven years the black-sailed ship came and took its hostages. The Athenians did not dare resist, for King Minos had declared that if they tried, he would send his great army to destroy all of Athens.

But one year, when the awful time came again, a great hero joined the band of captives who boarded the sad ship. It was Theseus, the prince of Athens. He stood on the deck beneath the black sails, and he set his eyes straight ahead as the ship plowed across the water toward Crete. For he had sworn to free his countrymen from this awful curse, or die trying.

When the ship reached Crete at last, Theseus stood with the others before King Minos.

"Who are you?" Minos demanded.

"My name is Theseus," the hero replied. "I am the son of the king of Athens. I have come to ask you to let me face the Minotaur alone. If I slay him, you must trouble the people of Athens no longer. If I fail, my companions will follow me into the Labyrinth."

"The king's son wishes to die." Minos laughed. "Very well. You will face the Minotaur tomorrow."

Now, it happened that Minos's own daughter, a wise and tenderhearted girl named Ariadne, saw the look of courage in the eyes of Theseus. That night, she crept past her father's guards and gave the prince a dagger.

"This will help you face the Minotaur," she whispered. "But even if you are strong enough to kill the monster, you will need to find your way out of the Labyrinth. It is made of so many dark twists and turns that not even my father knows the secrets of its windings. So you must also take this with you."

She placed in his hand a spool of gold thread, and told him to tie one end to a stone as soon as he entered the Labyrinth." Hold tight to the spool as you wander through the maze," she said. "When you are ready to come back, the thread will be your guide."

"Why are you doing this?" Theseus asked. "If your father finds out, you will be in great danger."

"Yes," Ariadne answered slowly, "but if I do not help, you and your friends will be in far greater danger."

And Theseus knew then that he loved her.

The next morning Theseus was led to the Labyrinth. As soon as the guards shut him inside, he fastened one end of the thread to a pointed rock, and began to walk slowly, keeping firm hold of the precious string. He wandered down the narrow hallways. He passed through many dark, winding passages, going farther and farther into the maze. Finally he reached a room heaped high with bones, and he knew he was very near the beast.

He heard a faint sound, like the echo of a roar. He stood still and listened. The sound came nearer and louder! Theseus stooped and quickly scooped up a handful of dirt, and with his other hand drew his dagger.

The roars of the Minotaur came nearer and nearer. Now his feet could be heard thudding along the floor. Theseus crouched in the shadows. His heart was beating quickly. On came the Minotaur. It caught sight of the crouching figure, gave a great roar, and rushed straight for it. Theseus leaped up and, dodging to one side, dashed his handful of dirt into the beast's eyes.

The Minotaur bellowed in pain. It tossed its great head up and down, and it rushed around and around, feeling with its hands for the wall. It was quite blinded by the dirt in its eyes! Theseus saw his chance. He crept up behind the monster and plunged his dagger into the beast. Down fell the Minotaur, with a crash and a roar, biting at the rocky floor with its lion's teeth. Theseus lunged at the monster, and drove his sharp knife through its heart. After that the Minotaur lay still.

Theseus breathed a sigh of relief, then took his dagger and cut off the monster's head. With this proof of victory, he followed the string through the winding, gloomy passages, until at last he came back to the beginning of the Labyrinth.

"I do not know what miracle caused you to come out of the Labyrinth alive," Minos said when he saw the monster's head, "but I will keep my word. I promised you freedom if you slew the Minotaur. You and your comrades may go."

Theseus knew he owed his life and his country's freedom to Ariadne's courage, and he knew he could not leave without her. Some say that he asked Minos for her hand in marriage, and the king gladly consented. Others say Ariadne stole onto the departing ship at the last minute without her father's knowledge. Either way, the two lovers were together when the anchor lifted and the dark ship sailed away from Crete.

Helen Keller's Teacher

Some of the luckiest boys and girls are the ones who have teachers as heroes.

Helen Keller was not like most little girls. She could not see the flowers blooming in her yard, or the butterflies floating from blossom to blossom, or the white clouds drifting in the high, blue sky. She could not hear the birds singing in the treetops outside her window, or the laughing and singing of other children at play. Little Helen was blind and deaf.

And because she could not hear people talking, Helen had never learned to speak. She could clutch her mother's dress and follow her around the house, but she did not know how to say to her, "I love you." She could climb into her father's lap, but she could not ask him, "Will you read me a story?" She lived in a dark, quiet world, where she felt all alone.

One afternoon when she was almost seven years old, Helen stood on her porch. She could feel a warm glow on her face, but she did not know it came from the sun. She smelled the sweetness of the honeysuckle vine growing beside her house, but she did not know what it was.

Suddenly Helen felt two arms wrap around her and hold her close. She knew at once it was not her mother or her father. At first she kicked and scratched and hit, trying to drive this stranger away. But then she began to wonder who it might be. She reached out and felt the stranger's face, then her dress, and then the big suitcase she carried with her.

How was Helen to understand that this young woman was Annie Sullivan, who had come to live with Helen and be her teacher?

Annie had brought a present. She gave Helen a doll. Then she put her fingers against Helen's hand, and made signs that Helen could feel. Annie slowly spelled D-O-L-L with her fingers. Helen felt Annie's fingers moving, but she did not know what this woman was trying to tell her. She did not understand that each of these finger signs was a letter, and that the letters spelled the word *doll*. She pushed Annie away.

The new teacher did not give up. She gave Helen a piece of cake, and spelled the word C-A-K-E against her hand. Helen made the signs with her own fingers, but still she did not understand what they meant.

Over the next days and weeks, Annie put many different things into Helen's hands, and spelled out the words. She tried to teach her words like *pin*, and *hat*, and *cup*. To Helen it all seemed very odd. She grew tired of this strange woman always taking her hand. Sometimes she grew angry with Annie, and began striking out at the darkness around her. She kicked and scratched. She screamed and growled. She broke plates and lamps.

Sometimes Annie wondered if she would ever be able to help little Helen break out of her lonely world of darkness and silence. But she promised herself she would not give up.

88

Then one morning Helen and Annie were walking outside when they passed an old well. Annie took Helen's hand and held it under the spout while she pumped. As the cold water rushed forth, Annie spelled W-A-T-E-R.

Helen stood still. In one hand she felt the cool, gushing water. In the other hand she felt Annie's fingers, making the signs over and over again. Suddenly a thrill of hope and joy filled her little heart. She understood that W-A-T-E-R meant the wonderful, cool something that was flowing over her hand. She understood at last what Annie had been trying to show her for days and weeks. She saw now that everything had a name, and that she could use her fingers to spell out each name!

Helen ran laughing and crying back to the house, pulling Annie along with her. She touched everything she could lay her hands on, asking for their names—*chair, table, door, mother, father, baby,* and many more. There were so many wonderful words to learn! But none was more wonderful than the word Helen learned when she touched Annie to ask her name, and Annie spelled T-E-A-C-H-E-R.

Helen Keller never stopped learning. She learned to read with her fingers, and how to write, and even how to speak. She went to school and to college, and Annie went with her to help her learn. Helen and Annie became friends for life.

Helen Keller grew up to be a great woman. She devoted her life to helping people who could not see or hear. She worked hard, and wrote books, and traveled across the seas. Everywhere she went, she brought people courage and hope. Presidents and kings greeted her, and the whole world grew to love her. A childhood that had begun in darkness and loneliness turned into a life full of much light and joy.

"And the most important day in my life," Helen said, "was the day my teacher came to me."

Father Flanagan

Here is the real-life story of a man who believed every boy needs a hero called father.

If you ever go to the state of Nebraska, you will find a very special town of children. The young citizens of this wonderful little village vote to elect their own mayor and council members, who might be boys or girls just a few years older than you. They hold their own court whenever someone breaks the rules. Like any city, their town has its own post office and fire station. It has schools, ball fields, movie theaters, and even its own town band.

This is the story of Father Flanagan, the man who founded such a marvelous place. He was born in Ireland, but when he was a young man he came to the United States to be a priest. His church was in Omaha, Nebraska, where our story begins.

Omaha had a problem—boys! Unlike most children, these boys had no mothers and fathers to look after them. Many of them had no homes, and no one to love them and show them right from wrong. And so, some of them got into trouble. They broke store windows, stole fruit from the grocer, and fought in the street.

When Father Flanagan saw their hungry faces and ragged clothes, it broke his heart.

"Those boys should be arrested," said the grocer. "They need to be taken away."

Father Flanagan shook his head. "What they need is a home," he said. "They need someone to love them."

"But who would take them in?" asked the grocer.

"Maybe I will," said Father Flanagan.

And he did. He borrowed a few dollars to rent an old house, and trudged from door to door, asking for used furniture, plates, cups, spoons, blankets, rugs, and anything else his neighbors would give away. When he told people what he was doing, they thought he was crazy. But they also saw a kind, good man and gave him what they could.

He started with just five boys and gave them a place to eat, sleep, play, and pray. He gave them a home where they could feel safe and warm.

This was just what they needed. Before long they were laughing, learning, and growing up strong. When people saw what Father Flanagan was doing, they brought him more homeless and orphan boys. Before long he had outgrown his house and had to find a bigger one. But more and more boys came, and soon they had outgrown the new house too.

"These boys need a place all to themselves," thought Father Flanagan, "where they can run and play in fresh air, go to school and church, and grow up to be fine young men. They need a town of their own."

And that is just what Father Flanagan gave them. Outside of Omaha he found a farm for sale. He had no money to buy the land, but that did not stop him. Once again he went to friends and neighbors for help. When they heard what he had in mind, they were puzzled. A town for boys nobody wanted? Whoever heard of such a thing? But they knew that when Father Flanagan got an idea, he would never give up. So they pitched in to help him buy the farm and build his town.

Before too long, the streets and sidewalks of Boys Town covered the fields. Father Flanagan and his friends built houses and shops. They built a church and a post office. They built a big dining room where all the boys could eat and a pool where they could swim. And from all over the country, boys without mothers or fathers to take care of them came to Boys Town, where Father Flanagan gave them a home.

One day a boy who could not walk came to Boys Town. He was a tiny fellow, so Father Flanagan asked one of the bigger boys to carry him to his room. The big boy hoisted the newcomer onto his back.

"He's not too heavy, is he?" Father Flanagan asked.

"He ain't heavy, Father. He's my brother!" The older boy smiled.

And that was the best thing of all about Father Flanagan's Boys Town. The boys who came there found a family of hundreds of brothers who took care of each other, and a father who loved them all.

Boys Town is still there today, and if you ever go to Nebraska, you can visit it and see it for yourself. The wonderful town is still full of boys—and girls now, too—who have no parents to take care of them. You can see them laughing, playing, and studying their books, and growing up to be strong, good people. And when you see the smiles on their faces, you can remember the story of the father who built the town so many children have called home.

The Hero of Indian Cliff

~ ADAPTED FROM C. H. CLAUDY

This is a story about true brotherhood, about putting yourself on the line for someone you love.

High above a valley floor, in the giant Rocky Mountains of Colorado, two brothers climbed a steep mountainside. Higher and higher they hiked, until it seemed they would reach the sky itself.

The older brother went first. He carried a knapsack of food, a canteen full of cold water, and a long coil of rope. Sometimes, when the trail grew very steep, he would tie the rope around a tree and throw the other end to his brother, to make it easier for him to follow.

"Get a good grip on the rope, Nando," he would call. "And watch where you plant your feet."

For a whole year, Nando had been waiting for this hike. Today he was nine years old. For a birthday present, his brother, Manuel, was finally showing him the way to a secret lookout—Indian Cliff!

Manuel was almost twelve, and he had been coming to Indian Cliff for two years now. He was sure of the path and could climb as quickly as a mountain goat. But today he went slowly, to help Nando along.

Sometimes Nando would try to climb too fast, and then he would lose his breath.

"Take your time, Nando," Manuel would say. "We'll get there soon enough."

Sometimes their feet knocked loose small stones, which went rolling down the mountain behind them. Nando could hear the echoes of the stones tumbling farther and farther away, crashing against trees or bouncing off boulders.

"Don't look down," Manuel would remind him. "Just keep your eyes on the trail."

Up and up they climbed. They passed behind a thundering waterfall. They hiked through woods where the trees clung to the rocks. They scrambled over ridges and inched their way through openings between huge boulders.

"I call this place Fat Man Squeeze." Manuel laughed, and Nando laughed too.

Finally they reached a place where the path grew level. They walked a short way through a forest. Then at once they left the trees and stepped into a small green meadow, perched on top of a towering cliff. It seemed as though the whole world lay at their feet.

Far, far below, Nando could see the valley where he lived. The highway running up the valley, the one his school bus followed every day, looked like nothing more than a thin black ribbon. His school seemed no bigger than a matchbox. Across the tiny woods and fields he could see his town, with its little streets and stores and steeples. And beyond the town lay more mountains, peak after peak capped with snow.

"This is it—my secret lookout," Manuel said. "I'll show you why I call it Indian Cliff." He reached into the hollow of a tree. When he pulled his hand out, it held three small sharp stones.

"Arrowheads!" Nando cried.

"Yeah. I found them lying on the trail," Manuel said proudly. "I think the Indians used to camp here."

The boys walked close to the edge of the cliff—but not too close—and found two rocks for seats. Manuel took sandwiches and apples from his knapsack, and they had lunch while they shared the view.

They ate without saying much. They did not want to spoil the wonderful silence that comes from being so far above the rest of the world. Together they watched the shadows of the clouds drifting across the valley floor, and followed the hawks and eagles floating far below them. They sat gazing for half an hour. At last Manuel stood up to stretch his legs.

Then it happened, without warning! The rock Manuel was using for a seat suddenly shifted. It slid down the slope toward the brink of the cliff, carrying Manuel with it!

Manuel gave a yell and spread out his arms, trying to catch hold of something. He felt himself sliding over the edge, and then falling. His feet struck a ledge, and he stopped—but at once the ledge crumbled away, and he felt himself sliding down again. His fingers grabbed on to a jagged bit of rock, and with a jerk he came to a halt.

He looked straight down and saw his legs dangling over empty space.

He was hanging from the side of Indian Cliff.

He did not try to move. In a flash he knew where his only hope lay.

"Nando!" he screamed. "The rope! Tie it around the arrowhead tree, and lower it down to me!"

Somewhere above he could hear Nando scrambling along the top of the cliff and calling down to him. A little bit of earth, loosened from above in some way, struck him gently on the shoulders and neck. What if a large amount should come down before Nando could get the rope to him?

"But it won't—I'm sure it won't. Nando will send the rope down in a minute—and then I'll get out of this mess," Manuel told himself. But then he had a horrible thought: *"What if the rope is not long enough to reach me?"*

Manuel's fingers ached. With each passing second, it grew harder and harder to hold on. He knew that any movement might cause him to lose his grip. But slowly, slowly he turned his head, and strained his eyes to look up. And far above, he caught sight of the end of the rope. Nando was lowering it down the cliff!

Manuel watched it come slowly down the rock face, twisting and turning like a long, thin snake. Moving slowly, sliding, catching on bits of rock and then dropping again, the end came gradually nearer. And then it stopped—just a few inches above Manuel's hands!

"It's no good!" Manuel yelled. "I can't reach it!"

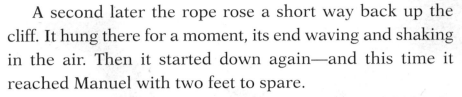

A second later the rope rose a short way back up the cliff. It hung there for a moment, its end waving and shaking in the air. Then it started down again—and this time it reached Manuel with two feet to spare.

Manuel held his breath, got a firm grip, and slowly began to pull himself up. He pulled with his arms, and pushed with his legs by sticking his feet into cracks in the cliff. Halfway up he had a terrible scare—the rope seemed to give a little, and at the same time he heard a cry from Nando somewhere above.

Now Manuel was only five feet from the top—now three feet—only one foot to go—now safety! With a shout of joy he pulled himself onto the top of the cliff.

At once he saw what Nando had done. His little brother lay on his stomach, his arms locked tight around the arrowhead tree. The rope was knotted around one of his ankles. There had not been enough rope to reach Manuel, so Nando had made it longer with his own body!

Manuel fell on the ground beside Nando, put one arm around his neck, and burst into sobs of relief. In a moment Nando sat up, and his face was shining with joy.

Nando's ankle was bruised and raw from the rope. Manuel helped him stand up and told him to lean on his arm. Together they started back down the trail toward home.

"I was scared, Manuel, real scared," Nando said.

"I know," Manuel answered. "I was scared too."

They walked slowly, helping each other along.

"And I know one more thing," Manuel said. "I'll never come back to Indian Cliff without my little brother to look after me."

Tashira's Turn

The small, daily examples of others can turn any one of us into a hero.

One day Tashira ran outside for recess and found her mother on the edge of the school yard with a bucket of soap and water. She was scrubbing a wall where someone had painted some ugly words and pictures. She scrubbed as hard as she could.

"Mama!" Tashira called. "What are you doing here?"

"Oh, I'm just helping your teachers keep the school clean," her mother said.

"It looks like hard work," said Tashira.

"It's nothing at all." Her mother smiled. "It's just my turn to help, you see."

The school bell rang. Tashira's teacher looked out the door and waved. Tashira's mom waved back, and went back to scrubbing the wall. All the ugly words and pictures ran to the ground, where they turned into puddles of silver and gold.

The next morning Tashira was walking past her church, when she heard voices singing in the sky. She looked straight up, and saw her teacher on the roof!

"Hello, Mrs. Jenkins," Tashira called. "What are you doing way up there?"

"We're helping our friend Reverend Wilburn," her teacher called down. "The steeple needs a fresh coat of paint."

"That's very brave of you to climb so high," Tashira shouted.

"It's not so very high," her teacher sang out. "Besides, it's our turn to help today."

Reverend Wilburn stepped out the church door and waved to his friends on the roof. Tashira's teacher waved her paintbrush back, and it looked as if she were painting the clouds in the sky.

The next morning, Tashira was skipping rope when she saw Reverend Wilburn with a basket under his arm.

"Hello, Reverend Wilburn," she called. "Where are you going with that great big basket?"

"I'm taking dinner to Officer Hamlette and his family." Reverend Wilburn smiled. "Mrs. Hamlette just had a new baby. Everyone in the church is taking turns sending a meal. Doesn't that smell good?" He lifted the basket's cover so Tashira could peek inside.

"It's very kind of you to cook such a nice, juicy turkey," she said.

"Oh, it's just my turn to help, that's all," said Reverend Wilburn.

He carried his basket up some steps and knocked four times. Officer Hamlette opened the door and smiled. Everyone on the street knew Officer Hamlette because he wore such a big, shiny badge. Inside the house, his brand new baby cried, and his smile grew wider than ever.

The next afternoon Tashira went to the park to play. But the swings were still and the slides were empty because a gang of bad boys stood on the corner, scaring the little children away.

Then Officer Hamlette came walking along with his big, shiny badge. When the bad boys saw him coming, they ran away. Officer Hamlette stood on the corner with his arms folded across his chest, watching them go. And before long, all the little children came out to play.

"Thank you for being so brave, Officer Hamlette," called Tashira. "We were scared to play until you came."

"Oh, it's nothing," smiled Officer Hamlette. "It's just my turn to help, that's all."

He stood on the corner all day long, making the playground safe until the mothers called the children home to their suppers. And even when the sun went down, and the shadows faded into dusk, Officer Hamlette stood under a streetlight, keeping the neighborhood safe.

The very next morning, Tashira was riding her bike when she heard a small voice crying. She looked and saw black smoke pouring out of an open window!

"Someone needs help," she told herself.

She jumped off her bike and ran to the window. The smoke stung her eyes, and she wanted to turn away. But she glimpsed a little boy inside.

"I want my mommy," he sobbed.

"I'll take you to her," Tashira told him. She reached through the window and pulled him out.

"Keisha's still there," he cried, pointing to the house.

Tashira looked back through the window. The smoke was so thick now, she could not see inside.

"Wait right here," she said. "We need more help."

Tashira ran down the street. A moment later she was back with Officer Hamlette running beside her.

Officer Hamlette disappeared into the smoke. Tashira waited and waited. He was gone an awfully long time. When he finally burst out of the house, he had a little girl in his arms.

Now the big fire engines roared down the street with their sirens screaming. The firemen jumped off the trucks. They dashed into the house with long hoses.

The children's mother came running. "Oh, my babies!" she cried.

Revered Wilburn came running. "Tashira, you're a hero!" he shouted.

Tashira's teacher came running. "She's a hero!" she shouted. "Tashira's a hero!"

A big crowd gathered around. Tashira's own mother was there to give her a big hug, too.

"You're a hero, Tashira!" they all shouted.

Tashira just shook her head and smiled. "I'm not a hero," she said. "It was just my turn to help, that's all."

But everyone said she was a hero, all the same.

When Mother Reads Aloud

*Children find heroes for life when mothers
and fathers read, "Once upon a time . . ."*

When Mother reads aloud, the past
Seems real as every day;
I hear the tramp of armies vast,
I see the spears and lances cast,
I join the thrilling fray.
Brave knights and ladies fair and proud
I meet when Mother reads aloud.

When Mother reads aloud, far lands
Seem very near and true;
I cross the desert's gleaming sands,
Or hunt the jungle's prowling bands,
Or sail the ocean blue.
Far heights, whose peaks the cold mists shroud,
I scale, when Mother reads aloud.

When Mother reads aloud, I long
For noble deeds to do—
To help the right, redress the wrong;
It seems so easy to be strong,
So simple to be true.
Oh, thick and fast the visions crowd
My eyes, when Mother reads aloud.